The All-American Soap Box Derby

A Review of the Formative Years 1938 thru 1941

RONALD R. REED

authorHOUSE®

AuthorHouse™
1663 Liberty Drive
Bloomington, IN 47403
www.authorhouse.com
Phone: 1 (800) 839-8640

Published by AuthorHouse   02/24/2016

ISBN: 978-1-5049-7722-7 (sc)
ISBN: 978-1-5049-7723-4 (hc)
ISBN: 978-1-5049-7721-0 (e)

Library of Congress Control Number: 2016901814

Print information available on the last page.

Any people depicted in stock imagery provided by Thinkstock are models, and such images are being used for illustrative purposes only. Certain stock imagery © Thinkstock.

This book is printed on acid-free paper.

Dedication

The person most deserving of thanks is my wife Sandy who has allowed me the time to pursue my passion and preoccupation with the derby.

Preface

The All-American Soap Box Derby

It's been billed as *the greatest amateur racing event in the world*. It's been called the *gravity grand prix,* but if you live in one of the cities which are hotbeds of soap box derby racing it is simply known as *the derby*. Large cities like Detroit, St. Louis, Cleveland and Atlanta and smaller ones like Anderson Indiana, White Plains New York and North Platte Nebraska have all had their share of success.

This is the third book in the series relating the story of this American tradition. The first, *Tallmadge Hill,* told of the inception of the race by creator Myron Scott, a newspaper photographer in Dayton Ohio. It followed the evolution of the race from a simple city race in 1933 to a national competition in 1934, and through its relocation to Akron in 1935. The second book, entitled *Derby Downs,* began with the construction in,1936, of the unique racing facility has been host to the All-American Soap Box Derby ever since. It chronicled the 1936 and1937 races.

This third book covers the next four years 1938 through 1941.

Acknowledgements

I wish to thank Dick Boye, Tex Finsterwald, Jeff Iula and Rick Acker for their generosity with their time, stories, advice and photos. Their insight and opinions have been most helpful. I would also like to thank all the librarians across the country for their assistance in searching for information used in this book. But mostly I owe a debt of gratitude to my granddaughter Teghan Reed who, at the age of 15, has become a marvelous secretary to me in assembling this book.

Introduction

The All-American Soap Box Derby, the brainchild of Dayton newspaperman Myron Scott, began as a local race in that city in 1933. With some creative promotion Scott turned it into a national competition the next year. By 1935 it had found a home in Akron. This move was solidified by the construction of Derby Downs. This unique facility, built in 1936, provided a much needed home. National sponsorship was provided by Chevrolet in cooperation with the Akron Beacon Journal and other newspapers across the nation. The All-American was flourishing due, in no small part, to the army of volunteers which enabled it run smoothly.

The Racing Format (Local)

Local races were run by the two division format. Class A included the older boys, while class B consisted of the younger ones. A champion would be determined in each class and the two winners would race in a heat for the city championship, with the winner going to Akron.

The Racing Format (All-American)

There was no age separation in the All-American finals in Akron. The national race was a single elimination race meaning lose once and you're done. Once the eliminations had reduced the field to nine cars, the following format was used; three heats of three cars each were run and the three champs who finish third in those heats raced in a heat to determine 7th, 8th and 9th places. Next, the three who finished second in those heats raced to determine 4th, 5th and 6th. And finally, the three winners of those heats competed in the championship heat. This format has been successful because it builds to a thrilling climax.

Part One

Prologue

The World in 1938

Internationally, Germany invaded Austria. In America the minimum wage was 40cents an hour and recession caused unemployment to reach nineteen percent.

Publishing giant Simon and Schuster was founded.

In science, the first public demonstration of color television took place in London. Nescafe gave Americans freeze dried coffee and DuPont introduced Nylon. The march of dimes was created to combat polio, and Seeing Eye dogs were being used for the first time.

In the world of politics, Joseph Kennedy was appointed ambassador to The United Kingdom.

The nation was scared out of its wits by Orson Welles as he broadcast a Halloween adaptation of the H.G. Wells story *War of the Worlds.*

Action Comics gave us Superman and Dennis the Menace also made his debut.

Aviator Douglas "Wrong Way" Corrigan left New York for Los Angeles and wound up in Ireland.

In the sports world, Floyd Roberts took the Indianapolis 500. The Kentucky Derby was won by Lawrin. In baseball Johnny Vander Meer pitched two consecutive no hitters in a five day period and the Yankees swept the Cubs in the World Series. In football the New York Giants reigned as NFL champs and TCU captured the same honor in the NCAA, going unbeaten in eleven games. In boxing, Joe Louis avenged an earlier defeat by knocking Max Schmeling out in the first round.

Hollywood gave us Snow White, Jezebel, The Citadel, Bringing up Baby, Boys Town and The Adventures of Robin Hood.

People were singing You Must have been a Beautiful Baby, Jeepers Creepers, September Song, A Tisket a Tasket, Thanks for the Memories and Whistle While you Work.

Notables born in 1938 include Natalie Wood, Kenny Rogers, Connie Francis, Evel Knievel, Oscar Robertson, Ted Turner, Charlie Pride and Jon Voight.

Two who died that year were Harvey Firestone and Clarence Darrow.

Leading up to the Race

In time for this year's race, additional grandstands were erected on the East side of the track, bringing the seating capacity at Derby Downs to 28,500. A tunnel was also built right under the track allowing easy access to this new seating from the parking lot. Now it was forbidden to cross the track during racing.

Due to economic hard times, thirty-three newspapers which had sponsored entrants in the 1937 race pulled out. At the same time twenty two new cities sent first time champs to this year's All-American. By this year problems in maintaining fairness and issues with the interpretation of the rules were on the increase. Some of the rules were relaxed in hopes of decreasing the complaints about "professional" assistance. Even so, officials had to delay thirty-five cars from racing until the boys themselves could make the necessary changes for their cars to comply with the rules.

James Kruer of Louisville was disqualified by race officials for having his father build his car, installing items like $28.00 wheel bearings. This price alone was more than the other champs had spent on their entire car.

This car was disqualified for illegal construction.

Five city champs in 1937 had brothers who won in the same city in 1938, four of them were:

Little Rock - Billy and Harold Kendrick

Omaha - Bill and Bob Berger

Bethlehem - John and Maurice Sigmans

Ft. Wayne – Dwight and Robert Davis

The fifth brother combination warranted special mention in this quote from the Akron Beacon Journal;

Beware, Racers! Another Ballard in Sunday Derby
White Plains Bob's Brother Richard Declared
Faster than Last Year's Champ

Ballard! A name to reckon with in soap box racing circles. Ballard is to the derby what Hartz and Shaw are to the Indianapolis speedway. And another Ballard is coming to town for the All-American Derby Sunday at Derby Downs. He is Richard Ballard, White Plains N. Y., and they say he is even faster than his brother Robert, who won everything in sight at the 1937 Derby, including the national and international championships. Robert's father, W. Lewis Ballard, a White Plains real estate dealer, said after the race last year that Akron would be seeing more of the Ballard brand of speed and added "I have a boy named Richard at home who is really faster than Bobby—only Bobby is oldest and his mother and I thought he should be the one to come. Lewis Ballard wasn't kidding. Richard won the derby sponsored by the White Plains Reporter and Sunday he will be out at the Downs determined to duplicate his brother's feat. His father is expected to accompany him to Akron as he was with Bobby last year.

Richard Ballard

Race Day

A host of radio personalities were on hand to broadcast the race over all the major networks. Indianapolis race car driver Harry Hartz was, once again, the flagman at the finish line. As always, Chevrolet sent advertising manager C.P. Fisken to welcome the champs to Akron and award the trophies and prizes at the banquet. Famous speedboat racer Gar Wood made his third trip to Derby Downs remarking that he didn't want to miss any of the fun.

Sunday before the race, Omaha champ Bob Berger approached Ed Stallsmith, chief inspector for the derby, with a question. "Is there anything in the rules which says I have to wear a racing shirt?" asked Berger. Informed that there was no such rule, Berger replied "Then I'm going to take mine off. I've got to pick up three tenths of a second somewhere, and I figure the sleeves of my shirt are acting like sails and holding me back." So Berger, who actually lived in Nebraska City, raced bareback all day.

Author's note:
I have recapped some of the more meaningful heats of each round, either by the part they played in determining the winner or by some interesting fact about the participants.

Round One

Heat 1

Lane 1 Stan Hartshorn Jr., Gardner, MA
Lane 2 Charles Porter, Bay City, MI
Lane 3 Jack Zordell, Benton Harbor, MI

In the first heat of the day, ten year-old Stan Hartshorn won by forty feet in his wood and tin orange racer. His winning time of 28.60 seconds was the day's fastest.

The first heat – also the fastest heat

Author's note:

Derby fans pay attention to the times recorded by the winners of each heat. When, during the day's racing, a new mark is set there is always a reaction from the crowd when the winning time is announced. This didn't happen in 1938 because the fastest time was set in the first heat and never bettered all day.

Heat 4

Lane 1 Melvin Paisley, Portland, OR
Lane 2 George Abel, New Haven, CT
Lane 3 Perley Bartlett, Portland, ME

Melvin Paisley, winner of heat four, was a boyhood pal of the Kendall brothers. Junior who raced in 1936 and Jack in 1937. These Portland champs had both placed in the All-American and Paisley's racer reflected their influence. Paisley later authored an autobiography called *Ace* in which he chronicled his exploits as a pilot in World War Two. George Abel's New Haven racer won the award for best brakes

The start of heat four

ACE!
Autobiography
Fighter Pilot WW II

By Melvyn Paisley
With Vicki Paisley

Paisley's book

Heat 5

Lane 1 Benjamin Cook, Nanticoke, PA
Lane 2 Milton Taylor, San Francisco, CA
Lane 3 Thomas Sjoblom, Knoxville, TN

A clean start to heat five

San Francisco scores an easy victory

Heat 8

Lane 1 Richard Butsch, Evansville, IN
Lane 2 Henry Higginbotham, Charleston, WV
Lane 3 Edward McLean, Boise, ID

Higginbotham was the first of many Charleston champs to finish in the money. He became a derby guru and for many years boys in Charleston came to him for construction tips.

Higginbotham increasing his lead

Heat 10

Lane 1 Clarence Hooker, Dover, OH
Lane 2 William Slocum, Macon, GA
Lane 3 Harold Wessinger, Columbia, SC

Wessinger's car defined the word *sleeper*. Called *The Coffin* no one thought it would do well. Although not pretty it was fast.

Start of heat ten

Heat 15

Lane 1 Loren Wiley, Mansfield, OH
Lane 2 Jack Wainwright, Springfield, IL
Lane 3 Edgar Bailey, Memphis, TN

This heat had no real bearing on the outcome of the race, but an interesting fact was that Bailey's car had zippers to close the cockpit.

The Memphis and Springfield Racers

Heat 21

Lane 1 George McClellan, Bristol, TN
Lane 2 Robert Berger, Omaha, NE
Lane 3 Richard Fish, Seattle, WA

The Omaha champ won going away, posting a winning time of 28.69 seconds, the second best of the day.

The start of Berger's first round heat

Heat 22

Lane 1 Robert Finlay, New York, NY
Lane 2 Michael Dreistadt, Scranton, PA
Lane 3 Robert Ransdell, Denver, CO

Finlay's red and silver speedster posted an easy win in heat twenty two.

Heat twenty two at the starting line

Heat 28

Lane 1 Lamar McDaniel, Atlanta, GA
Lane 2 Mark Splaine, Wausau, WI
Lane 3 Jack Roberts, Columbus, OH

Heat twenty eight winner McDaniel's mount was a masterpiece in construction.

They're off in heat twenty eight

Wilbur Shaw with Lamar McDaniel of Atlanta

Heat 31

Lane 1 Charles Abegg, North Platte, NE
Lane 2 Herbert Herrmann, Hawaii
Lane 3 Donald Anderson, Boston, MA

Anderson of Boston took the flag in this one. Another winner from New England

Boston on the way to a win

Heat 32

Lane 1 Robert Davis, Ft. Wayne, IN
Lane 2 Marion Trikosko, Kansas City, KS
Lane 3 Buddy Stroop, Panama Canal Zone

Kansas City's Trikosko scored a lopsided win in this heat, winning by twenty five feet.

Start of heat thirty two

Heat 33

Lane 1 Henry Hamilton, Sheridan, WY
Lane 2 Gerald Austensen, Battle Creek, MI
Lane 3 Jack Pennington, Detroit, MI

Pennington drove his checkerboard racer to victory in heat thirty three.

The starting blocks fall on heat thirty three

Heat 34

Lane 1 Charles Riedel, Carteret, NJ
Lane 2 Ralph Breckenridge, Akron, OH
Lane 3 John Kopf, Muscatine, IA

Akron's Breckenridge, who defeated 305 entries in the local race, drove a car that featured a hinged rear half that lifted up for easy entry. He was alone at the finish line.

The start of heat thirty four

and the finish

Heat 35

Lane 1 Charles Bourne, Erie, PA
Lane 2 Lawrence Tyler, Muncie, IN
Lane 3 Richard Ballard, White Plains, NY

The White Plains racer was the car everyone was waiting to see. There had been so much discussion about how fast he would be. After all, his brother had won last year, and his dad said this car was even faster. Young Ballard didn't disappoint as he won his first heat in the third best time of the day so far.

Ballard on his way to a first round win

At the conclusion of the first round the battle lines had been drawn. Only four times had the twenty nine second barrier been broken. The best marks were:

Hartshorn, of Gardner 28.60

Berger of Omaha 28.69

Ballard of White Plains 28.82

Higginbotham of Charleston 28.94

And three more boys had come close and could not be counted out, they were:

Trikosko of Kansas City 29.00

Finlay of New York 29.05

McDaniel of Atlanta 29.06

Round Two

There would be thirteen heats in this round

Heat 39

Hartshorn of Gardner won again, this time over Dallas and Cape Girardeau. His time was not nearly as fast as in the first round.

Heat 40

Lane 1 Melvin Paisley, Portland OR
Lane 2 Milton Taylor, San Francisco CA
Lane 3 Lynn Smith, Ann Arbor, MI

San Francisco's Taylor took heat 40 over Paisley of Portland. The third car in the heat was Lynn Smith of Ann Arbor.

San Francisco over Portland and Ann Arbor

Heat 41

The first boy to crack twenty nine seconds in the second round was Higginbotham of Charleston. He bested Philadelphia and Little Rock with a time of 28.99 seconds.

Harold Wessinger drove his *coffin* to victory in heat 42 over Tarrytown NY and Morgantown WV.

The *coffin* scores a win.

Doyle Bracewell of Des Moines had won in round one but his time was not impressive (29.42) He stayed alive, however with a second round win over Pottsville PA and Mansfield OH. He recorded a time of 29.43 in winning heat 43.

The only mishap of the day occurred in heat 44 as Allen Cloyd of Lexington racing in lane three lost control of his coaster and crossing into lane two crashed broadside into the car of Robert Holmes of Los Angeles driving him into the rail on the far side of lane one. Arthur Jacklin of Indianapolis escaped the mishap and won the heat in a good time of 29.03 seconds. After repairs were made to the car of Holmes he was allowed to race in a later heat.

Heat 45

Omaha's Berger took the lead a third of the way down the hill and was increasing it over Nashville and Anderson IN as he crossed the stripe in a time of 29.10.

Robert Kelly of Bloomington and Lazelle Grantham of Columbus GA, fell victim to New York's Robert Finlay in heat 46. He bettered his first round time with a posting of 29 seconds even.

In heat 47 it was a photo finish win over Tulsa by Maurice Sigmans of Bethlehem PA that kept his hopes alive. Maurice was the brother of John Sigmans who placed third in the 1937 All-American race. The third car in the heat was Worcester MA.

Worcester   Tulsa   Bethlehem

Heat 48

Lamar McDaniel recorded a 28.94 in beating Phil Savage of Flint by three and a half lengths. Far back in lane three was Thomas Sitler of Ellwood City PA.

Atlanta wins in round two

Heat 49

Kansas City and Detroit were eliminated by Donald Anderson of Boston.

The Beantown champ disposes of Kansas City and Detroit.

Richard Ballard had no trouble disposing of Akron's Breckenridge and Joe Bruno of Buffalo in heat 50, setting the fastest time of the round, a blistering 28.71 seconds.

White Plains eliminates Akron (Buffalo not shown)

Robert Holmes, the Los Angeles champ who was involved in the heat 49 mishap, was inserted into the last heat of the round. He was beaten by Robert Thompson of Marion IN, as was Jack Badorek of Peoria.

Only three champs recorded times under 29 seconds in the round, the fastest being Ballard's 28.71 followed by 28.94 by McDaniel and Higginbotham's 28.99.

The third round would really bring things into focus. Each third round winner would finish in the top six

Round Three

The third round, mostly two-car heats, went as follows:
Gardner over Charleston and San Francisco

Gardner's Hartshorn edges Higginbotham of Charleston

Columbia beating Des Moines
Indianapolis beaten by Omaha
New York besting Bethlehem
Boston falling to Atlanta
White Plains taking the measure of Marion

Round Four

The six finalists would race two at a time for a spot in the championship heat.

Stan Hartshorn of Gardner secured his place in the final with a win over Harold Wessinger of Columbia.

Next Omaha's Robert Berger punched his ticket to the big one with length and a half win over New York's Robert Finlay.

Berger (at bottom) wins over Finlay

Lastly, Richard Ballard joined Berger and Hartshorn by defeating Atlanta's Lamar McDaniel.

The championship heat was set. Ballard would race in lane one. Hartshorn would occupy lane two, with Berger in three. The crowd was equally divided on who would win. Berger had recorded faster times than Ballard in rounds one and three,

But Ballard had outdone Berger in rounds two and four. And don't forget Hartshorn had recorded the fastest time of the day in round one. This was going to be a terrific final.

The Championship Heat

The championship heat

From the other side of the track

The Mistake

The entire crowd stood as the starting blocks fell. For the first two hundred feet it was anyone's race. Then Ballard and Berger began to edge out to a slight advantage over the Gardner racer. In another ten seconds it became apparent that Hartshorn would finish third. As they shot across the finish stripe it was impossible to determine, with the naked eye, who had won. Even the trackside cameras couldn't determine a winner.

This would be a job for the photo- finish camera. After passing under the bridge spanning the finish line, Berger applied his brakes sooner than Ballard. The announcer, turning and seeing Ballard far ahead in the run out area, reacted to the illusion that the White Plains lad had crossed the finish line first. Forgetting the instructions to wait for official word from the judges, he announced that Ballard had won. As Ballard's racer came to a stop the car handlers immediately placed the car, with Ballard still in it, on the trailer to be returned to the finish line. Meanwhile the photo-finish picture was developed and it was readily apparent that a terrible mistake had been made. The staff on the bridge couldn't make themselves heard when they tried to get the announcer to correct the error. This lack of communication made for a chaotic scene. For those who knew that Berger was the actual winner, it was frustrating to see him sitting there alone in the dirt at the end of the concrete raceway. Meanwhile reporters were bombarding Ballard with questions and photographers were snapping countless pictures. He was just about to give his *thank you* speech when the announcement was made "There has been an error. The winner is not Richard Ballard but Robert Berger of Omaha." Still dazed and thinking he had won, Richard looked perplexed as a reporter came to him and said "That's tough luck, boy." "What do you mean?" He asked in a voice nervous with fatigue.

"I don't understand." It had taken two and a half minutes for the correct verdict during which he had lived a lifetime of emotions. He sat there for several minutes as the throng swept unheeding by him to get to Berger. Then he ran, as fast as he could, to his mother up in the stands. There were tears in Mrs. Ballard's eyes as she clasped her son in her arms and whispered the things only a mother knows how to say at a time like this. "Good sport son" she said. "You did just fine. After all, we don't want to be greedy in our family, do we?" She was referring to the fact that Richard's older brother Bob, had won the previous year. The crushing blow was eased by the fact that he would receive a new Chevrolet for placing second.

this photo was taken at the instant the announcer
was informed of the mistake.

For Berger the racing went on. There was still the international
championship to settle.

Lane 1 Buddy Stroop Panama Canal Zone
Lane 2 Robert Berger Omaha, NE
Lane 3 Bob Wilson Belleville Ontario, Canada

As expected neither Stroop nor Wilson posed a serious challenge to Berger as he breezed to an easy victory.

the start of the International championship

And the finish

At the giant post- race banquet the prizes were awarded and they were plentiful.

The first order of business was the special award trophies, fastest heat, best design, best brakes and best upholstery. Next were the top six placers.

(I have added the next four based on winning times) And additionally I have listed three who just missed placing.

The top five

The next five

Three racers just missed making the top ten.

Best Designed Thomas Sitler - Ellwood City

Maunce Sigmatis - Bethlehem

Doyle Bracewell - Des Moines

Best Brakes George Abel - New Haven

Robert Thompson - Marion

these cars came close to placing

Sidelights

In 1937 Bob Berger's brother Bill won the Omaha race. In Akron he was beaten in the second round by eventual world champ Bob Ballard. In 1938 the Berger family returned the favor when Bob Berger edged Dick Ballard in the championship heat. He later received the double honor of meeting Detroit Tiger star Charlie Gehringer and famed aviator Douglas "Wrong Way" Corrigan.

In a real oddity, Atlanta placed fifth in the All-American three years in a row. Tom Howard started it all in 1936 and in 1937 Hugh Flury carried on the trend. In 1938 Lamar McDaniel made it a trifecta with another fifth place showing. In 1938 seventeen small towns sent boys to race in the Atlanta local race.

Nine year old Chicago champion Tom Drije lost his mother three months prior to the race. He and dad Miles Drije plunged themselves in building his derby car to ease the pain of their loss.

In November of 1942 Life magazine published a ten page feature on Robert Berger who as an eighteen year old was a student at Nebraska University contemplating entry onto the armed service during World War two.

Berger in Life

Third place winner Stan Hartshorn fashioned his racer using a wooden door as the floorboard and wood scraps as framework. A tin sign that once advertised Glenwood cook stoves was used as covering. Hartshorn continued his education at Michigan University. Marrying in 1952, he and wife Sally raised six children. He lived to the age of eighty three. His car has been preserved and is currently on display at the Gardner Museum in Gardner MA.

Stan Hartshorn

For some unknown reason, there was no heat to determine fourth, fifth and sixth places. These spots were awarded based on the times recorded by Finlay, McDaniel and Wessinger in the fourth round.

Part Two

The World in 1939

The biggest international news was the invasion of Poland by German forces.

On a happier note, Batman made his debut in comic books.

In sports the Kentucky Derby was won by Johnstown. In baseball, the World Series was no contest as the Cincinnati Reds were swept by the powerful New York Yankees. The NCAA football championship was won by Texas A. & M.

Hollywood had its best year ever, producing such classics as Of Mice and Men, Wuthering Heights, The Hunchback of Notre Dame, Goodbye Mr. Chips, Ninotchka, Stagecoach, The Wizard of Oz, Young Mr. Lincoln and topped off by Oscar winner Gone With the Wind.

Notables born this year include Lee Majors, Marvin Gaye, Tina Turner, Sal Mineo, Neil Sedaka, Lee Harvey Oswald and David Frost.

Those who passed away include Amelia Earhart, Sigmund Freud, Zane Grey, Douglas Fairbanks Sr. and 1938 Indianapolis 500 winner Floyd Roberts.

Soap Box Derby Happenings

In preparation for the 1939 race, the annual rules meeting was held in October of 1938, and local newspaper representatives were invited. The newspapers ran the local derbies and paid for shipping the local winning car to Akron. They also paid the travel expenses for the local champ, his family and the local director. In recognition of this support, the rules committee invited the newspaper representatives. The committee felt that the papers should have firsthand knowledge of the reasons behind any rule changes. Also, the committee would benefit from feedback on problems at the local level. Despite this flattering invitation, there was another large turnover in sponsorship for the 1939 Derby.

Twenty-four newspapers discontinued sponsorship, but twenty-two papers in other cities sponsored champs for the first time. And, two cities returned to the competition after a year's absence. Finances certainly influenced a newspaper's decision. But sometimes there were other factors. Occasionally, when a local champ was disqualified at the All-American for violating a construction rule on his car, the supporting paper would be offended and decide not to have a race the next year. Regrettably it is generally believed that Chicago, Los Angeles and New York City, to name a few, each withdrew from the Derby for several years at various points in its history because of disqualifications.

The rule changes were few but noteworthy. Age limits were set at 10 to 15 year olds. The 250 pound weight limit remained, but a 150 pound maximum was set for the car alone. Cost limits were set at $7.00 for wheel and axle sets, and $10.00 for the rest of the car. Also test runs for all entrants at the finals were made mandatory.

The Track

The track at Derby Downs was generally much higher, steeper and longer than the tracks or streets on which the local races were held. And since the contestants were building better and faster cars each year, the speeds were now approaching and passing 40 miles per hour. Officials worried more and more about safety. There was talk of shortening the track to lower the speeds.

Local Races

One hundred twelve cities including two in Canada and one in the Panama Canal Zone staged races and sent their local champs to Akron for the sixth annual All-American Soap Box Derby.

Race Day

The date for the event was Sunday, August 13th. The weather forecast called for mostly sunny with a chance of rain late in the day. Notables on hand included the highly respected race driver Harry Hartz who was back to flag the heats at the finish line for the fifth straight year. Wilbur Shaw, fresh off his third victory in the Indianapolis 500, spent derby week welcoming and talking to the boys. And at the microphone to broadcast the race to the nation was one of the top sportscasters in America, Ted Husing.

Did He Build It?

Jim Schlemmer of the Akron Beacon Journal recounted the events of 1939.

"Cliff Hardesty won the White Plains, NY race and within two weeks 52 letters of protest were received at derby headquarters in Akron. The writers complained that no boy could possibly have built the superb car that Hardesty drove. When the car arrived, two days ahead of the boy, it was given quick and intense scrutiny by the rules board and technical committee in Akron. It looked like it might have rolled off an assembly line at Cadillac or Chrysler. It was radical in design, particularly in the matter of suspension, and it was as fine a piece of workmanship as one could ever hope to see. The body was entirely laminated. Even the interior was perfectly finished. There was doubt in the minds of the officials that it was boy-built.

When Hardesty arrived in Akron he turned out to be a cherubic boy of eleven weighing only sixty-two pounds and with the grandest smile and most captivating personality imaginable. He met, nevertheless, with a rather chilly reception despite the temperature which was flirting with the ninety degree mark. A jury of a dozen men, editors of the American Boy, Boy's Life, Popular Mechanics, Popular Science; Mechanics from Akron's Hower Vocational High School and members of the derby technical committee went into session with the boy, insisting upon considering him guilty until he proved himself innocent. For three hours on a hot sultry Friday night, in an airless room off the M. O'Neill Co. auditorium, the jury intentionally misconstrued and misinterpreted Cliff Hardesty's answers to expertly phrased questions. The jurors, persistent, puffing, perspiring and perplexed, kept at him until midnight. Then little Hardesty said, as cool as all get-out: 'Gentlemen, you forgot to ask me how did I balance my wheels.' That was too much. The jury sent him back to the Mayflower Hotel and to bed, with orders to be awake for continuance of the investigation in the morning. Saturday morning Hardesty was taken to an old garage on N. Summit Street where a lot of machinery had been dumped preliminary to the setting up of a National Youth Administration work shop. The room was a mess; some stuff was junk, some machinery had been uncrated and set up. Hardesty was given a pad and pencil and told to fill out requisitions for the material and tools he needed. He was then told to duplicate the front axle suspension on his car. He went right to work. Half an hour later the jurors stopped him. Humble and apologetic they were, too. Hardesty had done a better job than was to be found on the Soap Box Derby car which bore the White Plains name. "I'm sorry" Said Cliff, "but I don't quite get the feel of some of these tools and lathes. If I were in my own workshop back home I think I could have done a better job." That afternoon Hardesty cracked up during a drivers' test run at Derby Downs. He landed in the hospital. The car was wrecked. Through the afternoon and all that night some of the great technical minds of this nation, and the finest mechanics, worked ceaselessly to rebuild Cliff Hardesty's car. They finished on Sunday morning, only hours before the All-American championship races were to start. At noon a much-patched up boy was released from the hospital, his racing uniform hiding bandages which in turn hid most everything but his smile and twinkling eyes.

Hardesty after winning in White Plains

Round One

Heat 1

Lane 1 Fred Fisher, Detroit, MI
Lane 2 David Gabbert, Tacoma, WA
Lane 3 Edwin Jesse, Nashville, TN

Although comparing winning times from one year to another is pointless, due to conditions at the track changing, Chevrolet, however, made a special note each time a new track record was set. Herbert Muench set the standard of 28.20 seconds in 1936, and no one bettered this mark in 1937 or 1938. In 1939 Fred Fisher of Detroit eclipsed that record in the first heat of the day, recording a time of 28.11. In heat seven, Charleston's Warren Harmon erased that mark with a 28.04. Ten minutes later, in heat fourteen, Terre Haute champ Jack Harkness cracked the 28 second barrier rolling up a time of 27.90. This record stood for exactly ninety seconds as Cliff Hardesty set the fastest time of the day at 27.80 seconds in the very next heat.

Author's note: Remember the name Fisher, of Detroit. It will come into play later.

Fred Fisher

Heat 4

Lane 1 Keith Vincent, Battle Creek, MI
Lane 2 Tom Watson, Chicago, IL
Lane 3 Paul Johnson, Madison, WI

Paul Johnson's car was judged the best upholstered but he lost to Keith Vincent in the first round.

Start of heat four

Heat 6

Lane 1 Arthur Nelson, Des Moines, IA
Lane 2 Harlan Bursh, Minneapolis, MN
Lane 3 L. J. Bussey, Council Bluffs, IA

Bursh won by half a length with a decent time of 28.15 seconds.

Heat 7

Lane 1 Warren Harmon, Charleston, WV
Lane 2 Richard Disalvi, Trenton, NJ
Lane 3 Julien Rattelade, Durham, NC

Harmon scored an easy win in 28.04 seconds.

Charleston's first heat

Heat 13

Lane 1 Raymond Poccia, Mamaroneck, NY
Lane 2 Ed Bamber, Manchester, NH
Lane 3 Jack McDonald, Seattle, WA

The photo finish camera was needed to determine the winner of this heat. This would happen several more times.

Photo finish

Heat 14

Lane 1 Richard Byler, Marion, IN
Lane 2 Jack Harkness, Terre Haute, IN
Lane 3 Jack Roberts, Washington, PA

Harkness was the first to crack the 28 second barrier.

Harkness in lane two

Heat 15

Lane 1 Clifford Hardesty, White Plains, NY
Lane 2 Jack Weihl, Marietta, OH
Lane 3 Gene Kindinger, Mansfield, OH

Hardesty recorded the fastest time of the day in winning heat 15, a blistering 27.80 seconds.

Hardesty's first heat

Heat 18

Lane 1 Charles O. Titus Jr., Portland, ME
Lane 2 Robert F. Lane, New York, NY
Lane 3 Ed Geer, Peoria, IL

This race resulted in a dead heat between Peoria and Portland. In the rerun, Portland prevailed.

Author's note: All three cars participated in the rerun. Today, only the two cars which tied would compete in the run off.

The start of the dead heat

The photo finish of the rerun

Heat 21

Lane 1 Dean Bailey, Memphis, TN
Lane 2 John Jones, Scranton, PA
Lane 3 William Lofft, Philadelphia, PA

It became evident very early that Bailey of Memphis was one to watch. He won easily, and his winning time of 28.00 seconds was outstanding.

An easy win for Bailey of Memphis

Heat 23

Lane 1 Raymond Nourse, Newark, OH
Lane 2 Roy L. Yelverton, Raleigh, NC
Lane 3 Mason Colbert, North Platte, NE

Colbert became an instant favorite in a racer which was more streamlined than most of the others. He took heat 23 easily with a time of 27.90 seconds.

North Platte in lane three

Heat 33

Lane 1 Ronald Hoskins, Donora, PA
Lane 2 Charles Tubbs, Akron, OH
Lane 3 Joe Cook, El Paso, TX

Although hometown hopeful Charles Tubbs was alone at the finish line, his time was a mediocre 28.40 seconds. The high school sophomore consistently had the fastest times in winning the Akron race a week earlier.

Akron's "Scoopy" Tubbs in lane two

Heat 34

Lane 1 Arthur Taylor, Bowling Green, KY
Lane 2 Charles Cunningham, San Francisco, CA
Lane 3 Thomas Watson, Newport News, VA

San Francisco was another one to watch.

Heat 35

Lane 1 Benjamin Evans, Columbus, OH
Lane 2 Jack Doney, Kalamazoo, MI
Lane3 Lewis Spessard, Hagerstown, MD

As heat 35 left the starting blocks rain began to fall. It increased steadily and by the end of the first round (heat 38) it was a downpour and racing was suspended in the interest of safety. After a thirty five minute delay the rain finally stopped and racing resumed with second round action. The wet track caused times to be slower by about one half second. The track did not dry evenly. Certain parts remained wet longer than others. This made time comparisons unreliable.

Rain begins to fall

Round Two

There were no close heats in round two. The thirteen winners all won by at least a full car length.

Round Three

Heat 52

Lane 1 Warren Harmon, Charleston, WV
Lane 2 Fred Fisher, Detroit, MI
Lane 3 Harlan Bursh, Minneapolis, MN

The third round consisted of six heats and began with Harmon besting Bursh and Fisher in the only three-car heat of the round.

Charleston beats Detroit and Minneapolis

The other five were two-car heats. This would bring the number of boys remaining to six. His winning time of 28.71 showed the effect of the wet track.

The next three heats were easy wins for Hardesty, of White Plains, Bailey of Memphis and North Platte's Colbert. Each won by such a large margin that only the winning cars could be seen in the photo finish pictures.

A dejected Washington DC champ Carl Cedarstrand
is sad after losing to Mason Colbert of North Platte.
Colbert's car is shown in the background.

Heat 56

Lane 1 Harold Armstrong, Kansas City, KS
Lane 2 Charles Tubbs, Akron, OH

The times posted by the contestants in the first two rounds seemed
to indicate that Armstrong would win easily. As they hit the finish stripe
the partisan crowd hoped for an upset, but no one could tell for sure. The
front axle on The Akron car appeared to cross the line first. Did the long
nose of the Kansas City racer edge ahead at the last second? It was clearly
a task for the photo finish camera. The picture, when developed, showed
that they had hit the stripe at the exact same instant. The heat would have
to be rerun.

the start of the dead heat

So back to the starting line they went. Again it took a photo to determine a winner. This time Armstrong nipped Tubbs by the narrowest of margins.

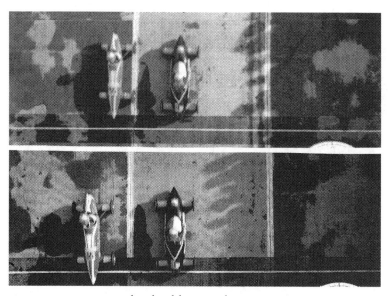

the dead heat and rerun

In the final heat of the round Charles Cunningham of San Francisco scored an easy win over Wilbur Ballard of Buckhannon WV.

Round Four

Six champs remained to vie for the crown, six great cars, driven by six hopeful boys. The round would consist of three two-car heats. The three who placed second in each heat would race for fourth, fifth and sixth, and the three winners would go into the championship heat. (This would all change.)

Heat 58

Lane 1 Cliff Hardesty, White Plains, NY
Lane 2 Warren Harmon, Charleston, WV

The round began routinely enough with Hardesty besting Harmon by six feet. His margin would have been bigger, but he didn't drive very well and edged over into lane two.

Hardesty winning over Harmon

Heat 59

Lane 1 Mason Colbert, North Platte, NE
Lane 3 Dean Bailey, Memphis, TN

This heat would have a profound effect on the rest of the day. The Memphis racer crept out to a small lead of one foot but then Bailey began to have trouble controlling his white car. This allowed Colbert to take the lead. He steadily increased his lead and won by a half car length. Then things turned bad! Fifty feet beyond the stripe Bailey applied the brakes. As he did so his tiny car swerved crazily. It plowed straight into the tail of the Nebraska comet then slammed into the kickboard lining the track, taking Colbert's with it. Both boys were thrown from their seats onto the concrete. Bailey slid along on his back which was badly scraped. Colbert was not badly injured. But the worst news was that both cars were damaged beyond repair. Colbert, by nature of his win was awarded third place and Bailey sixth.

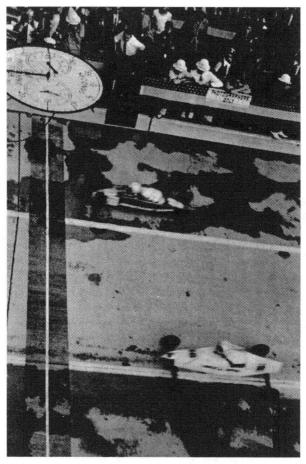

A split second later- disaster

Heat 60

Lane 1Charles Cunningham, San Francisco, CA
Lane 2 Harold Armstrong, Kansas City, KS

Armstrong qualified for the championship heat with a five foot victory over Cunningham.

a win for Kansas City

Heat 61

Lane 1Warren Harmon, Charleston, WV
Lane 2 Charles Cunningham, San Francisco, CA

With sixth place awarded to Dean Bailey, this became a two- car heat for fourth and fifth place, and Harmon prevailed. No known photos of this heat exist.

The Championship

Heat 62

Lane 1 Clifford Hardesty, White Plains, NY
Lane 2 Harold Armstrong, Kansas City, KS

With Colbert's award of third place the championship heat became a two-car affair.

Author's note:

Hardesty was assigned lane one and Armstrong lane two. Nowadays this would not happen. In the interest of safety two- car heats are now run in lanes one and three.

With the collision and, subsequent awarding of third place, much of the drama was removed from the championship heat. While Armstrong had raced well, his times were not among the fastest of the day. The final heat did not appear to be evenly matched, and it wasn't. Soon after the starting blocks fell Hardesty began to pull away from the Kansas City champ. By the time they crossed the finish line his lead had increased to ten feet. The crown responded with a warm ovation as the White Plains lad was brought back to the finish line and presented his All-American winner's trophy.

The start of the championship heat

and the finish

Hardesty is the winner

The International Championship

Heat 64

Lane 1 Clifford Hardesty, White Plains, NY
Lane 2 Harvey Wright, Colon, Panama
Lane 3 Ernest Young, Belleville Ont.

Neither Wright nor Young proved to be any challenge to Hardesty as he cruised to a thirty foot win over Wright with Young another forty feet back. Hardesty was now truly the world champ of derby racing. He and Wright, while still in their cars, were loaded onto the trailer and brought back to the finish line for photos, interviews and the awarding of trophies.

Start of the international heat

And the finish

The Question

The conclusion of the race program left a huge question unanswered. "Could Colbert have beaten Hardesty?" A comparison of times for both boys fails to settle the debate. Cliff's black beauty set the all-time fastest heat on Derby Downs in the first round when he clocked a 27.80 seconds. Colbert in that first round brought his car across the finish line in 27.90. When rain fell at the beginning of the second round, and a breeze blew intermittently up the track, times were inconsistent and Hardesty recorded a 28.36 while Colbert ran a time of 28 seconds flat. In the third round Cliff again had the faster time 28.46 to Mason's 28.50. But Colbert's ill-fated last dash was timed in 28.25 against Cliff's 28.37. Thus each boy can claim two heats faster than the other. So the question remains and we will never have an answer.

Hardesty vs Colbert - The question remains.

The Banquet

Books were piled on Hardesty's chair so he could be seen on the dais at the banquet.

Hardesty collected a lot of hardware.

While Chevrolet awarded placing trophies to only the top six boys, I have taken the liberty of designating seventh through ninth spots based on the best winning times.

The final tally goes as follows:

1st Clifford Hardesty – White Plains NY
2nd Harold Armstrong – Kansas City KS
3rd Mason Colbert – North Platte NE
4th Warren Harmon – Charleston WV
5th Charles Cunningham – San Francisco CA
6th Dean Bailey – Memphis TN
7th Harlan Bursh – Minneapolis MN
8th Charles Tubbs – Akron OH
9th Carl Cedarstrand – Washington DC

The special awards
Fastest Heat - Hardesty
Best designed - William Gettig Benton Harbor MI
Best Brakes - Charles Tubbs Akron OH

Best Upholstery - Paul Johnson Madison WI

Hardesty, Armstrong, Colbert, Harmon,
Cunningham, Bailey, Bursh and Tubbs

Sidelights

Los Angeles Champ Bill Griffiths was on crutches due to an injury to his knee suffered at home.

The dead heat between Armstrong of Kansas City KS and Akron's Charles Tubbs was the third in derby history. This would occur several more times through the years.

In the fall Chevrolet exhibited the placing and award winning cars at its facility in Detroit.

Chevrolet's derby exhibit in Detroit

Part Three

The World in 1940

In international news Russian Bolshevik leader Leon Trotsky was assassinated while in exile in Mexico. German troops invaded Denmark and Winston Churchill was named Prime Minister of England.

In America, the first social security checks were issued, the Pennsylvania turnpike opened as did the first McDonald's restaurant (in Pasadena). The Pulitzer Prize went to John Steinbeck for. *The Grapes of Wrath.*

In the world of entertainment WNBT in New York became the first regularly operating television station. Making his debut on radio was Superman and the first cartoon featuring Bugs Bunny also appeared.

In baseball, the Cincinnati Reds defeated the Detroit Tigers four games to three to take the World Series. The NCAA football champs were the Minnesota Gophers and Kentucky downed Kansas to become the basketball champs. And Gallahadion won the run for the roses in Louisville.

The Oscar for best movie went to Rebecca with Jimmy Stewart copping the best actor award for The Philadelphia Story. The best actress was Ginger Rogers in Kitty Foyle.

Notables born in in 1940 include Raquel Welch, John Lennon, Tom Jones, Ricky Nelson, Ringo Starr, Alex Trebek and Richard Pryor. Soccer star Pele, Gene Pitney, Wilma Rudolph, Jack Nicklaus and Mario Andretti.

Those who passed away include Cowboy movie star Tom Mix, British Prime Minister Neville Chamberlain and author F. Scott Fitzgerald.

The Rules

The biggest change instituted by the rules committee was the exclusion of ten year-olds from competition since a large percentage of mishaps lately had involved the youngest drivers. Wheel bearings not built specifically for Derby wheels were forbidden as were free floating axles. These axles rotated with the wheels supposedly with less friction but they had so much free play they were regarded as unsafe. Since smaller boys in smaller cars were winning, rule makers wanted to give an equal chance to bigger boys whose bigger cars suffered from greater wind resistance. To supplement the 1939 decision that set the 150lb. limit for the car alone, the rules now forbid the use of added weight. Some smaller boys had been meeting the 150 lb. limit on the car itself then adding weight on race day to bring the total car plus boy weight up to the 250 lb. limit. Forbidding the use of added weight, officials thought, would negate the advantage of the smaller boy in the smaller car.

Changes at Derby Downs

Several physical changes took place at Derby Downs to increase safety and visibility. Early in July construction began on a new permanent grandstand on the east side of the track to match the west grandstand. To compensate for the increasing speed of the cars, and to keep the speeds around 35 mph, officials shortened the racing distance to 1,000 feet. They moved the starting line down the hill 100 feet, eliminating the steepest portion of the track, and they relocated the finish line 75 feet up the hill. This required also moving the bridge. The west grandstand was moved 21 feet further back from the track to improve the spectators' sight lines. The construction, this year, of Akron's new municipal stadium, The Rubber Bowl, immediately east of the course just beyond the finish line, added a large area of new pavement to the run out area. The 36,000 seat venue cost $750,000 and took one year in construction. It was home to Akron University football for sixty nine years (324games). Its history included over 1,500 high school games, including state playoffs, countless concerts including Simon and Garfunkel, The Rolling Stones, Aretha Franklin and Rod Stewart.

In late July and early August, 128 American cities held local races and sent their champs to Akron along with one from Canada and another from the Panama Canal Zone. On Thursday of Derby week first champ to arrive in Akron was Jesse Urban of Santa Fe New Mexico. Most of the others came in on Friday. They all came with one thought in mind, to become the world champ. Most made a beeline for the M. O'Neil department store in downtown Akron where the cars were being displayed. The cars reflected the many hours of hard work needed construct a winner. What a dazzling assortment of shapes, sizes and colors! Saturday the champs took their test runs in alphabetical order and that night they were honored as part of the official opening of the Rubber Bowl. The dedication attracted a, standing room only, crowd of 37,000.

Derby Day

August 11th dawned sunny and hot. The forecast called for showers. The necessary adjustments had been made and the test runs had been taken. One hundred thirty cars sat poised at topside. The huge crowd filed in anticipating a great day of racing. They were not disappointed. The six former world champs posed for a group photo, decked out in their matching outfits provided by Chevrolet.

Turner, Bale, Muench, Ballard, Berger and Hardesty

Wilbur Shaw was on hand as he had been all week. Of course Harry Hartz would handle the job of flagman at the finish line, as he had every year since 1935. Also present was all six of the past world Derby champs, each wearing a smart blue blazer and white trousers furnished by Chevrolet. As the giant prerace parade began, the spectators checked their programs to learn the heat in which their favorite champ would be racing in the first round. As the parade marched by the grandstand the champs received a fine ovation. Each one carried a flag emblazoned with the city he was representing. Upon the completion of the parade, the crowd stood as a local high school band played the national anthem. With all the preliminaries over it was time for racing.

Author's note: Once again I have included only the heats which had a bearing on determining the winner or contained an interesting fact. Since the track had been shortened, any comparison to previous years' times would be pointless.

Round One

Heat 2

Lane 1 Ray Hudachek, Iowa City, IA
Lane 2 Ian Webber, White Plains, NY
Lane 3 John Gage, Manchester, NH

With the fantastic success White Plains had enjoyed, it came as a shock when the city's representative, Ian Webber, was beaten by Ray Hudachek of Iowa City who recorded a winning time of 26.64 seconds.

Heat two brought a surprise

Heat 4

Lane 1 Don Pfeiffer, Sonora, CA
Lane 2 Thomas Bruno, Niagara Falls, NY
Lane 3 Vaughn Williams, Dallas, TX

Pfeiffer recorded a good time of 26.95 seconds in winning heat four.

Pfeiffer was in lane one

Heat 7

Lane 1 John Young, Indianapolis, IN
Lane 2 Richard Stamegna, Mamaroneck, NJ
Lane 3 Paul Rustwick, Sioux City, IA

Start of heat seven

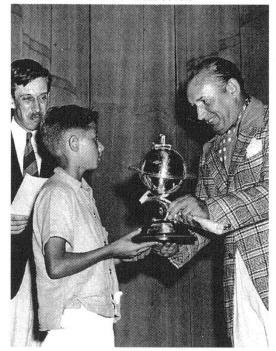

Upon winning the local race in Mamaroneck Richard Stamegna was presented his trophy by Robert Ripley of Ripley's Believe it or Not. He was beaten in heat seven by John Young of Indianapolis.

Heat 8

Lane 1 William Walters, New Brunswick, NJ
Lane 2 Jack Butler, Wabash, IN
Lane3 Thomas Fisher, Detroit, MI

Tom Fisher broke his older brother Fred's track record in winning the local race in Detroit. He and Fred worked during the winter months on design, and began construction in early spring. He won his first heat in convincing fashion recording the third winning time under 27 seconds.

Tom Fisher of Detroit

Heat 11

Lane 1 John Porter, North Platte, NE
Lane 2 Donald Chance, Ironton, OH

Lane 3 Walter Hollingsworth, Charlotte, NC

Fifteen year-old John Porter who actually lived in Nebraska City set the fastest times in winning the North Platte city race. After capturing the championship, he ran an exhibition race against Mason Colbert, the 1939 North Platte champ who placed third in Akron. In winning that race he set a faster time than in the regular competition.

Porter in lane one

Heat 12

Lane 1 Ralph Schnur, Orlando, FL
Lane 2 Clifford Johnson, Chicago, IL
Lane 3 Donald Davenport, Tacoma, WA

The city race in Chicago drew 700 entrants. Eleven year-old Harvey Stair took the championship by defeating Clifford Johnson in the final heat. In Akron on Thursday evening of Derby week, Stair's racer was disqualified, by the inspection committee, for illegal construction. He would have to try again next year. The need arose to find the second place winner to represent the windy city in Akron. All day Friday the sponsoring Chicago newspaper sought to find young Cliff Johnson and his car. Lo and behold it was discovered that the Johnson family was already in Akron to watch the race. There was still the problem of getting Cliff's car here in time for inspection and a trial run. It was locked in Grandfather Leo Becker's basement 300 miles away in Peoria. After securing permission from the Beckers to break into the basement (they were on vacation) the car was rescued and sent by express to Akron. Young Johnson was beaten in heat thirteen by Donald Davenport of Tacoma.

Cliff Johnson in lane two

Heat 19

Lane 1 Gordon Kiester, Pontiac, MI
Lane2 Carl Yelverton, Raleigh, NC
Lane 3 Richard Huling, Marietta, OH

Kiester rolled up a good time in winning heat 19.

Kiester in lane one

Heat 24

Lane 1 Ray Steeves, Wichita, KS
Lane 2 John Lamb, Gary, IN
Lane 3 Edward Pendo, Deadwood, SD

Steeves won in a car which featured a tail fin

Steeves in lane one (note tail fin)

Heat 29

Lane 1 Robert Londeree, Charleston, WV
Lane 2 Hartell Saugman, San Francisco, CA
Lane 3 Robert Froehner, Muscatine, IA

Charleston's Londeree took heat 29 in a well styled yellow racer which made good use of its windshield.

Londeree's racer was a honey

Heat 30

Lane 1 Robert Travis, Nashville, TN
Lane 2 Dean Stielow, Des Moines, IA
Lane 3 Hubert Summerford, Montgomery, AL

Stielow set the fastest time of the first round, a 26.57 mark.

Wilbur Shaw and Dean Stielow

Heat 41

Lane 1 E.L. Adams, Hazard, KY
Lane 2 George Smith, Akron, OH
Lane 3 Harlan Williamson, Jacksonville, IL

Hometown champ George Smith recorded six times under 27 seconds in winning the Akron local race a week earlier. He cruised to an easy victory in heat 41.

Smith in lane two

Of the forty four first round winners exactly half recorded times under twenty seven seconds. The second round would consist of fifteen heats.

Round Two

Times were even better in the second round as twelve of the fifteen set times under 27 seconds. Donald Pfeiffer rolled up a new low of 26.40 in heat forty seven only to have it broken in the very next heat. In heat forty eight Tom Fisher's dash down the track was timed at 26.30 seconds for the fastest heat of the day.

The fastest heat of the day

Heat 59

Lane 1 William Hull, Hagerstown, MD
Lane 2 George Smith, Akron, OH
Lane 3 Walter Wenck, Chattanooga, TN

George Smith was adding to his lead as he crossed the finish line.

another win for Akron's Smith

Heat 60

Lane 1 Ted Matzke, Scottsbluff, NE
Lane 3 Frank Keefe, Tucson, AZ

Three hundred feet past the finish line Ted Matzke, who had won the heat, sideswiped the Tucson car and overturned. He received a lacerated arm and shoulder.

Round Three

This round would determine the six finalists.

Heat 61

Lane 1 Raymond Hudachek, Iowa City
Lane 2 Donald Pfeiffer, Sonora, CA
Lane 3 Thomas Fisher, Detroit, MI

Detroit's Tom Fisher continued his quest for the championship with a third round win over two good cars.

The photo finish picture of heat 61

Heat 62 saw North Platte's John Porter defeat George Bach of Philadelphia

Heat 63 Kiester of Pontiac cruised to a win over Ray Steeves of Wichita and Norbert Rehm of Fort Wayne.

Heat 64 Charleston hopeful Robert Londeree prevailed over Thomas Anderson of Muncie IN.

Heat 65 Ivan Davis representing Kansas City KS edged Richard Naser of Washington PA and LeRoy Wilkerson of Columbus GA.

It was announced that George Smith desired to wait until Matzke, who had the mishap in heat 60, felt better before running heat 66. After a ten minute delay, Matzke regained his bearings and the heat was run. Smith scored a two car length victory over Matzke.

Round Four

Now six cars remained. The round would consist of three heats with two cars in each. The three cars which were beaten would race for fourth, fifth and sixth. The three winners would vie for the championship.

Heat 67

Lane 1 John Porter, North Platte
Lane 3 Thomas Fisher, Detroit

Porter gave Fisher his biggest challenge of the day in this heat.

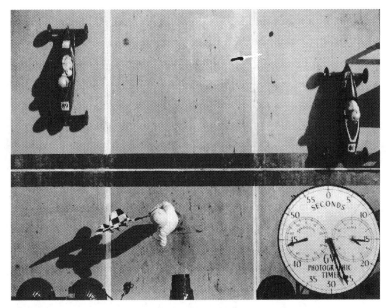

Fisher edges Porter

Heat 68

Lane 1 Gordon Kiester, Pontiac
Lane 3 Robert Londeree, Charleston

It took the photo finish camera to determine the winner in this one. The Charleston car edged Pontiac by less than a foot for the win.

Londeree nips Kiester

There is no photo available of heat 69 in which George Smith of Akron won over Kansas City's Ivan Davis

Round Five

Now the lineups were set. The race for fourth, fifth and sixth would go as follows:

Heat 70

Lane 1 John Porter, North Platte
Lane 2 Ivan Davis, Kansas City
Lane 3 Gordon Kiester, Pontiac

In the closest heat of the day Kiester edged Porter for fourth place.

Pontiac, Fifth - North Platte, Sixth- Kansas City

The All-American Championship

Heat 71

Lane 1 Robert Londeree, Charleston, WV
Lane 2 George Smith, Akron, OH
Lane 3 Thomas Fisher, Detroit, MI

As the three cars sped down the track, only a foot or two separated each of them. At the midway point the Detroit News car added to its advantage until Fisher crossed the finish stripe nearly a full car length ahead of Londeree with Smith another six inches further back.

The Photo finish of the final

The final heat from the bridge

Having captured the All-American championship Fisher would next take on the foreign champs in the International race.

Heat 72

Lane 1 Thomas Fisher, Detroit, MI
Lane 2 Donald McGowan, Belleville, Ont.
Lane 3 Teddy Stewart, Colon, Canal Zone

This heat was a total mismatch as Fisher won by at least ten car lengths.

no contest
Indianapolis 500 drivers Harry Hartz and Wilbur Shaw congratulated
Tom Fisher on five heats of great driving

Hartz, Fisher and Shaw

The Banquet

The champs and their parents sat down to a fine meal followed by a few speeches from the Chevrolet executives. Thankfully the talks were brief and the program moved along with the awarding of the trophies and prizes. The 1,200 in attendance sheered as each participant received a gold watch and a racing diploma. Each got to keep his official racing garb, helmet and goggles.

The special award for best design went to Mark Bratton of Pampa Texas

Frederick Jennings took the trophy for best brakes, and the best upholstered car was that of Ralph Schnur of Orlando Florida. Of course the fastest heat trophy went to Fisher. The top six place winners received large trophies. They were:

First – Thomas Fisher, Detroit
Second – Robert Londeree, Charleston
Third – George Smith, Akron
Fourth – Gordon Kiester, Pontiac
Fifth – John Porter, North Platte

Sixth – Ivan Davis, Kansas City

The winners

To these I have added:
Seventh – Ray Hudachek, Iowa City
Eighth – Donald Pfeiffer, Sonora
Ninth – George Bach, Philadelphia
Tenth – Ray Steeves, Wichita

Sidelights

With cramped foot room in the nose of his car, Tom Fisher had trouble operating the brakes with his shoes on, so he ended up driving to victory in his stocking feet.

In his six heats he was pressed only once, when he beat fifth place finisher John Porter by three feet.

Robert Londeree was a model of consistency. While his times were good, they were not great. He didn't record a winning time among the ten best. But he kept on winning. The only racer he couldn't beat was Fisher

Gordon Kiester drove his blue speedster to a fourth place finish recording the fifth fastest time of the day. Kiester who spent $9.97 constructing his car eliminated eight other champs before being edged in a photo finish by Londeree.

Seventh place finisher Ray Hudachek made quite a name for himself in the business world. His engineering vocation took him to Germany, Puerto Rico and Saudi Arabia. He passed away at the age of eighty five after a full and rewarding life.

Lawrence Massachusetts champ Don Condon's mother was struck by a derby car as she ran onto the track in Lawrence. She made the trip to Akron despite a broken ankle. In the All-American, Condon scraped the kickboard and came to a stop ten feet from the finish line.

Ft. Wayne IN, Muncie IN, Washington PA, Columbus GA and Scottsbluff NE just missed being among the top nine.

As was the practice since 1936, Chevrolet set up an October derby display in the General Motors building in Detroit, featuring the winning cars.

Chevrolet's derby display

Ohio led the way with fourteen cities represented; Pennsylvania had thirteen, followed by New York with twelve and Indiana with ten.

Part Four

The World in 1941

In international news, Germany continued its assault on the surrounding countries invading one after another. The British navy sank the German battleship Bismarck. On the 7th of December, 353 Japanese planes attacked Pearl Harbor killing 2,403 people. The following day, President Roosevelt declared war on Japan.

On the home front, Mt. Rushmore was completed. General Mills introduced Cheerios and Chanel #5 made its debut. Finally, Bob Hope performed the first of countless USO shows.

In horseracing, Eddie Arcaro won the Triple Crown aboard Whirlaway. In baseball, Ted Williams was the last major leaguer to hit over .400 and Joe Dimaggio hit safely in 56 consecutive games, a record that still stands.

In basketball, the NCAA champs were the Wisconsin Badgers and in boxing, Joe Louis defended his heavyweight title seven times.

The Oscar for best picture went to *How Green was My Valley*. Gary Cooper took best actor honors for *Sargent York* and Joan Fontaine won best actress for *Suspicion*. Other notable movies were, *Citizen Kane, The Maltese Falcon,* and Walt Disney's *Dumbo*.

The tunes of the day were Take the A Train, by Duke Ellington, Everything Happens to me, by Frank Sinatra and Chattanooga Choo Choo by Glenn Miller.

Notables born this year include Martha Stewart, Neil Diamond, Paul Simon, Ann- Margaret, Jesse Jackson, Faye Dunaway and Chubby Checker. Those passing away were Lou Gehrig, James Joyce, Virginia Woolf and Helen Morgan.

Leading up to the race

There was a large turnover in cities represented in the race. Among the twenty which withdrew were Denver CO, El Paso TX, Kansas City KS, Nashville TN and Raleigh NC. The sixteen cities to join or return to racing included Hudson NY, Reno NV, Salt Lake City UT and Williamsport PA.

The last champ to arrive in Akron was John Koudelka of Minneapolis. (See heat 17.)

During his trial run Ann Arbor's Richard Ohlinger swerved near the finish line tearing the rubber off the wheels of his racer. They were replaced and he was back in business.

The city of Akron staged a gigantic rededication of the Rubber Bowl stadium on the night before the race. Forty thousand fans, including the derby champs, packed the facility for the celebration. The festivities included bands, color guards, circus acts, fireworks and a stirring rendition of Battle Hymn of the Republic by Metropolitan Opera star Mary Van Kirk.

The NBC radio network, with Tom Manning and Lynn Brandt would broadcast the race, as would Bill Griffiths for the Mutual network.

The giant prerace parade featured fourteen bands, several color guards and majorette units. The seven former world champs rode in convertibles and the 117 city champs dressed in their bright racing togs marched proudly down the track. Each champ carried a flag emblazoned with the name of the city he represented. The last band in the parade stopped under the finish line bridge to play the National Anthem. With the festivities concluded, it was time for racing.

The racing helmets used in 1940 were manufactured, in England, exclusively for the Derby. They were modeled after the ones worn by drivers in the Indianapolis 500 race, complete with visors and goggles. In

1941 the British ship bringing the new ones to the states was torpedoed and sunk by a German warship and the entire cargo was lost somewhere in the Atlantic Ocean. Chevrolet hurriedly purchased silver Minnesota style football helmets which were decorated with Chevrolet's BODY BY FISHER logo on the front and the city of each contestant on the side.

Round One

The Preliminary Heats

Author's note: I have recapped the more meaningful heats and the ones which contained a story of interest, omitting the ones which had no bearing on how the winner was determined.

Heat 1

Lane 1 Donald Stamm, Portland, OR
Lane 2 Thomas Hollingsworth, Charlotte, NC
Lane 3 Robert Burnham, Cincinnati, OH

The photo finish equipment was tested early as the first race of the day ended in a dead heat between Stamm and Hollingsworth. For the rerun, the Charlotte car was moved to lane three. **This is never done today!** Hollingsworth edged Stamm in the rerun.

The start of the dead heat

Heat 3

Lane 1 Douglas Sawdey, Iowa City, IA
Lane 2 John Ferguson, Hazard, KY
Lane 3 Douglas Vinson, Dallas, TX

Iowa City's Doug Sawdey experienced difficulty controlling his car and failed to finish after hitting the kickboard on the east side of the track. This was particularly disappointing since Iowa City had placed seventh, the previous year, in a similar car. Vinson of Dallas captured the heat.

Doug Sawdey shows his disappointment

Heat 6

Lane 1 Joseph Harbin, Anderson, IN
Lane 2 Donald Nichols, Ft. Wayne, IN
Lane 3 Jack Elliott, Little Rock, AR

Ft. Wayne's Don Nichols got the attention of the crowd with a winning time of 26.73 seconds. He was the first champ to record a time under 27 seconds.

Nichols wins heat six

Heat 7

Lane 1 Eugene Johann, Benton Harbor, MI
Lane 2 Franklin Halley, Columbus, OH
Lane 3 Donald Teghtmyer, Wichita, KS

Teghtmyer easily took heat seven in a red racer that was a masterpiece in design. It was very low and narrow, with an ideally shaped cockpit. The boy and car fit each other perfectly. While the paint was not glossy, the car was built for speed. As any boy will tell you, pretty paint does not win races. This heat proved to be the day's fastest, a remarkable 26.46 seconds.

Wichita wins (at bottom) the fastest heat

Heat 14

Lane 1 Gene Bean, Washington, DC
Lane 2 Carl Price, Bloomington, IN
Lane 3 Jerome Chapman, Juneau, Alaska

The gentle breeze, that blew intermittently, affected times. When Gene Bean won heat fourteen, his winning time was a mediocre 27.31but it was the third best of the day to that point.

Gene Bean's racer

Heat 15

Lane 1 Calvin Smiege, Madison, WI
Lane 2 William White, Detroit, MI
Lane 3 Paul Linehan, Glens Falls, NY

In winning the Detroit local race Bill White 13, of Royal Oak, eclipsed the record time set in 1940 by Tom Fisher who went on to win the world championship at Akron. Traveling the 650 foot course he shaved 4/5 of a second off Fisher's record. Needless to say the large contingent of Detroit derby rooters had high expectations. Young Bill took his first heat with ease.

White in lane two

Heat 17

Lane 1 Jack Koudelka, Minneapolis, MN
Lane 2 John McDaniels, Charleston, WV
Lane 3 John Good, Athens, OH

Although John McDaniels won heat seventeen with a good time of 27.24 seconds, there is another fascinating story connected with this race. John Koudelka, who represented Minneapolis, spent a year in bed at age thirteen, due to rheumatic fever. His father brought him a deck of cards and a book on magic to help him pass the time. Soon he was hooked. Honing his craft as an adult, he became one of the best magicians in the world. He headlined in Las Vegas and on the Ed Sullivan Show. Having changed his name, he was now billed as Jack Kodell and he performed for the Queen of England and Winston Churchill. He gained fame by incorporating live parakeets in his act, and performing while on ice skates. He enjoyed a long and rewarding career and published his autobiography entitled *Do Something Different*. He passed away in 2012.

The start of heat seventeen

The magic of Kodell

Heat 22

Lane 1 Donald Matthews, Albany, NY
Lane 2 Richard Davis, Sonora, CA
Lane 3 Robert Hurt, Charlottesville, VA

Richard Davis was in Akron trying to better the mark set by 1940's Sonora champ Don Pfeiffer who placed eighth. He got off to a great start by winning heat twenty two with a good time of 27.13

Another good Sonora racer

Heat 25

Lane 1 Richard Foote, Champaign-Urbana, IL
Lane 2 Edw. Keenan, Oil City PA
Lane 3 George Pinkel, Franklin, NJ

Richard Foote's racer featured a radical windshield treatment.

Foote's racer

Heat 31

Lane 1 Kirk Stetson, Rochester, NY
Lane 2 Robert Enterline, Harrisburg, PA
Lane 3 Thomas Hagood, Orlando, FL

Stetson, the son of an Eastman Kodak engineer represented Rochester New York. He handily captured heat thirty one. The front axle did not go through his car but was attached out front. As an adult, Stetson taught mathematics and physics in Istanbul, Turkey. He passed away in November of 2012.

Stetson winning

Heat 32

Lane 1 Henry Buch Jr., Woodstock, IL
Lane 2 Wesley Holmes, Boston, MA
Lane 3 Mendal Turner, Muncie, IN

Mendal Turner was the younger brother of Bob Turner, the winner of the first All-American Soap Box Derby in 1934. He was edged in his first heat by Wesley Holmes of Boston.

Mendal Turner

Heat 35

Lane 1 Robert Mosher, Beloit, WI
Lane 2 Ronald Clayton, Terre Haute, IN
Lane 3 Claude Smith, Akron, OH

Akron was pinning its hopes on fourteen year old Claude Smith. His brother George had placed third nationally in 1940 and Claude had set consistently fast times in winning the Akron city race over a field of 273 contestants. He applied twelve coats of enamel to his speedster, painstakingly sanding the surface between each coat. The car weighed 119 pounds and cost $9.50 to build

Akron's Smith wins by a large margin.

To summarize the first round, only three champs recorded winning times better than twenty seven seconds. Donald Teghtmyer of Wichita led the way with his 26.46. Second was Akron's Claude Smith at 26.64 and the other was Ft. Wayne champ, Don Nichols, rolling up a 26.73 seconds.

Round Two

The second round would consist of thirteen heats. With the slower racers eliminated, the average times improved.

Heat 45

Lane 1 Gene Bean, Washington, DC
Lane 2 Jack Vaughn, Indianapolis, IN
Lane 3 William White, Detroit, MI

The large group of Detroit rooters saw their hopes for back to back All-American champs dashed as Gene Bean eliminated Bill White in a close race.

White Vaughn Bean

Heat 46

Lane 1 George McGraw, Chicago, IL
Lane 2 John McDaniels, Charleston, WV
Lane 3 William McKown, San Antonio, TX

John McDaniels established himself as a favorite with a winning time of 26.87 seconds.

Chicago   Charleston   San Antonio

Heat 47

Lane 1 Robert Schantis, San Francisco, CA
Lane 2 F.A. Forgione, Niagara Falls, NY
Lane 3 William Zoller, Cleveland, OH

In winning heat 47, Zoller showed the largest improvement in his winning time. His 26.93 was a half second faster than his first round time of 27.43 seconds.

Zoller in lane three

Heat 51

Lane 1 Kirk Stetson, Rochester, NY
Lane 2 Wesley Holmes, Boston, MA
Lane 3 Roger Patterson, Batavia, NY

Kirk Stetson nearly cracked the 27 second barrier in winning heat 51. His time was 27.02 seconds.

A view of heat 51 looking down the track

Heat 52

Lane 1 Claude Smith, Akron, OH
Lane 2 R. Beaulas, Holyoke, MA
Lane 3 George Runck, North Platte, NE

Smith recorded the fastest time of the second round, 26.64 seconds, as he won his heat easily.

Akron   Holyoke   North Platte

Summarizing the second round, eleven of the thirteen winners bettered their first round times. Five set times under 27 seconds. The three fastest were Akron, Charleston and Cleveland.

Round Three

This round would consist of six heats, one heat of three cars and five heats of two. This would determine the six finalists.

Heat 54

Lane 1 Donald Teghtmyer, Wichita, KS
Lane 2 Thomas Hollingsworth, Charlotte, NC
Lane 3 Donald Nichols, Ft. Wayne, IN

This heat pitted the boy with the fastest heat against the champ with two times of less than 27 seconds, and the one who had run a dead heat and won the rerun. Nichols of Ft. Wayne scored a surprisingly easy victory.

An easy win for Nichols

Heat 55

Lane 1Donald Webber, White Plains, NY
Lane 3 Gene Bean, Washington, DC

Although White Plains had done remarkably well in previous years, this year it was not to be. Bean prevailed in a heat which was not close. Donald Webber was the brother of Ian Webber, the 1940 White Plains champ.

Heat 55 just out of the starting blocks

Heat 56

Lane 1John McDaniels, Charleston, WV
Lane 3 William Zoller, Cleveland, OH

In the most thrilling race of the round McDaniels edged Zoller in a photo finish. The Charleston champ displayed driving which was a bit erratic, crossing the finish line out of his lane. This would prove costly later.

The photo finish of heat 56

In the last three heats of the round went as follows:

Richard Davis of Sonora defeated Dale Snyder of Woodbury NJ

Kirk Stetson representing Rochester NY won over Mamaroneck NJ's Renato DiVito.

Akron's Claude Smith bested Laurence Sherman the Syracuse NY champ.

Round Four

This was the positioning round. It would consist of three two-car heats. The three losers of these heats would race for fourth, fifth and sixth, and then the three winners would compete in the championship heat.

Heat 60

Lane 1 Don Nichols, Ft. Wayne

Lane 3 Gene Bean, Washington, DC

This was the biggest upset of the day. Nichols had posted faster times than Bean in each of the three rounds, but the little champ from the nation's capital edged the Midwestern champ at the finish. As the saying goes, that's why they run them.

Washington DC upsets Ft. Wayne

Heat 61

Lane 1 John McDaniels, Charleston
Lane 3 Richard Davis, Sonora

McDaniels edged his orange racer across the finish line to take the heat but his elation was short lived. He lost control just past the stripe and smashed into the wooden kickboard lining the track. The impact did extensive damage to the body and wheels of his mount. It would require large scale repair. Thankfully he was not injured. The car, along with McDaniels, was loaded on the trailer and returned to the topside repair pits. The mournful champ watched sadly as the topside crew rushed to restore it to racing condition. Three hundred West Virginians including most of the boys who raced in Charleston had come to Akron to cheer him on. Dozens of champs offered their wheels or anything else needed to repair the damage.

An ill-fated heat for Charleston

Heat 62

Lane 1 Kirk Stetson, Rochester
Lane 3 Claude Smith, Akron

Much to the delight of the partisan crowd, the hometown champ scored an easy win. The margin of victory was three car lengths. For the third time Smith had recorded the fastest winning time of the round. Akron, like Charleston, would be in the final heat for the second straight year.

Round Five

The Semi-Final

Heat 63

Lane 1 Nichols, Ft. Wayne
Lane 2 Stetson, Rochester
Lane 3 Davis, Sonora

The crowd was on its feet as the starting blocks fell. For the first two hundred feet it was anyone's race. Then Stetson, in lane two, began to lag a bit. At the halfway point Nichols and Davis were still neck and neck with Stetson trailing. Then Nichols crept out to a slight edge, and as they swept across the finish line, the Ft. Wayne speedster had opened up a lead of eighteen inches. Stetson had faded in the home stretch and finished two lengths back.

4th Ft. Wayne, 5th Sonora and 6th Rochester

The Championship Heat

Heat 64

Lane 1 Smith, Akron
Lane 2 McDaniels, Charleston
Lane 3 Bean, Washington, DC

After a ten minute delay, to complete the repairs to the Charleston car, the heat was set. Smith cruised to a surprisingly easy ten foot win over McDaniels with Bean another car length back. Claude never wavered from the center of his lane. In fact he drove perfectly in all five of his heats, recording a time under twenty seven seconds in each one. Akron had waited eight long years for this day, and the celebration was deafening.

The start of the final

and the finish

McDaniels watches repair work on his car

Claude Smith comforts a disappointed John McDaniels.

The next order of business was the International Championship.

Heat 65

Lane 1 Douglas Bone, Belleville, Ont.
Lane 2 Claude Smith, Akron, OH
Lane 3 Eduardo Benton, Mexico City

As usual the International Championship heat was not much more than a curtain call for the All-American champion. The foreign champs provided no competition for Smith but the race gave the crowd another chance to cheer for their champ.

The start of the International heat

And the finish

As the happy crowd filed out of Derby Downs the laughing, chatting, sunburned fans had no idea that they would not see another derby race for five years. With the attack on Pearl Harbor and the onset of World War II, Chevrolet decided to concentrate its effort on war production. In a letter sent to all the newspapers in the participating cities, the automobile manufacturer stated that the derby would be suspended, and be continued when conditions warranted its resumption. The biggest shame was that many young boys, across the nation, who had fallen just short in their efforts to win local races, would not get another chance.

At the annual awards banquet at the Akron Armory, the trophies scholarships and other prizes were distributed in grand fashion. After a fine meal and a few short speeches by Chevrolet executives, the prize distribution began. Each participant received a Waltham wrist watch and racing diploma. Also each got to keep his racing garb, racing helmet and goggles. The next order of business was the special awards. The blue racer of Ashland's Ramon McMillen was judged best upholstered. New York's William Hewitt won for best brakes with his bright red car. Copping the award for design was Billie Davenport of Des Moines. His black beauty featured a large windshield. And the fastest heat was recorded by Donald Teghtmyer of Wichita.

The Placers

The top six looked like this:

FIRST	Claude Smith	Akron	
SECOND	John McDaniels	Charleston	
THIRD	Gene Bean	Washington DC	
FOURTH	Don Nichols	Ft. Wayne	
FIFTH	Richard Davis	Sonora	
SIXTH	Kirk Stetson	Rochester	

To this I have added:

SEVENTH	William Zoller	Cleveland	
EIGHTH	Don Teghtmyer	Wichita	
NINTH	Tom Hollingsworth Charlotte		

The top six- Smith, McDaniels, Bean, Nichols, Davis and Stetson

The Winning Cars

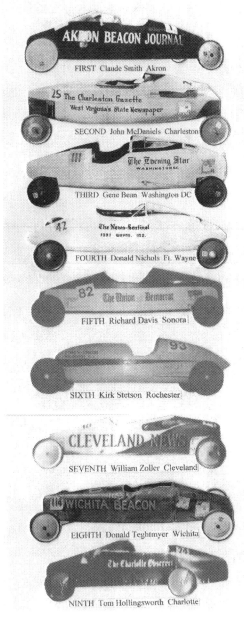

The placers

UPHOLSTERY Ramon McMillen Ashland

BRAKES Wm. Hewitt New York

BEST DESIGN Billie Davenport Des Moines

The special award winners

An artist was commissioned to create a likeness of each of the world champs and he did a remarkable job for many years

34 Turner   35 Bale   36 Muench   37 Ballard

38 Berger   39 Hardesty   40 Fisher   41 Smith

A good looking group of boys

Sidelights

Claude was the son of a machine operator at the Goodyear Tire and Rubber Co. and a sophomore at Akron's Kenmore High School. It was his fourth try at winning the Akron race. It took him nearly nine months to build his car.

The tallest champ was Harold Zoellner of Cape Girardeau MO who stood six foot two. The smallest was George Pinkal who hailed from Sussex New Jersey and weighed sixty nine pounds.

Boston champ Wesley Holmes was an identical twin. He defeated his brother Warren in his hometown race.

Mendal Turner, younger brother of the 1934 world champ Bob Turner, won in Muncie. He didn't fare well in Akron, however, losing his first round heat.

New York and Ohio led the way in representation. Each had twelve cities in the race. Next came Indiana with ten, followed by Pennsylvania and Michigan with nine and eight respectively.

The International Championship heat was discontinued after 1941. It had been a mismatch every year and added nothing to the program. Foreign champs raced in the regular competition beginning in 1946.

Claude Smith, his mother and brother traveled to New York to appear on the Voice of Firestone radio program. Mrs. Smith commented that it would feel strange not to have the basement a mess due to derby car construction.

As in past years, an autumn derby display at Chevrolet in Detroit featured all the winning and special award cars.

Epilogue

At the conclusion of the war Chevrolet, true to its word, resumed the All-American Soap Box Derby. In 1946 it came back bigger and better than ever. Of course through the forties and fifties there were changes, many of which added to the pageantry. Celebrities from the world of movies sports, television, and politics added to the fun. The champs spent most of Derby Week at Derbytown, a camp nearby where they swam, rode horses, played sports and had cookouts. The celebrities visited camp and took part in the activities. There were also changes on race day. In 1950 the Oil Can Trophy Race was instituted whereby three famous stars of the day raced in comic cars prior to the actual competition, and the winner's trophy was in the shape of a gigantic oil can. The winner in this inaugural race was former heavyweight champion Jack Dempsey who defeated Jimmy Stewart and Wilbur Shaw.